PICTURE LIBRARY

SUBMARINES

PICTURE LIBRARY
SUBMARINES

C.J. Norman

Franklin Watts

London   New York   Sydney   Toronto

© 1986 Franklin Watts Ltd

First published in Great Britain
   1986 by
Franklin Watts Ltd
12a Golden Square
London W1R 4BA

First published in the USA by
Franklin Watts Inc
387 Park Avenue South
New York
N.Y. 10016

First published in Australia by
Franklin Watts
14 Mars Road
Lane Cove
2066, NSW

UK ISBN: 0 86313 350 9
US ISBN: 0–531–10091–X
Library of Congress Catalog Card
Number: 85–51455

Printed in Italy

Designed by
Barrett & Willard

Photographs by
British Aerospace
BUE SubSea
ECP Armées
Fleet Photographic, Royal Navy
Royal Navy Submarine Museum
Naval Photographic Center, Washington DC
Secretary of Defense, Pentagon
Vickers Oceanics
Westland Helicopters

Illustration by
Janos Marffy/Jillian Burgess Artists

Technical Consultant
Bernard Fitzsimons

Series Editor
N.S. Barrett

Contents

Introduction

Submarines are vessels that can operate under water. Most work as part of a nation's navy. In wartime, they attack enemy ships and submarines. Special submarines are equipped with nuclear missiles, each powerful enough to destroy a city.

Some undersea craft are used for peaceful purposes, such as exploring the sea bed or repairing cables. These are usually called submersibles.

△ Crewmen at the controls of the USS *Ohio*, a ballistic missile submarine. The *Ohio* came into service in 1981. It was the first of its class and much larger than previous submarines.

The biggest submarines are propelled by nuclear power. Those that can launch nuclear missiles from under the sea are called ballistic missile submarines. Submarines used for attacking ships and other submarines are called hunter-killers.

Smaller submarines run on diesel fuel. These are less expensive to build. They are sometimes called patrol submarines.

△ USS *Michigan* is an Ohio-class submarine. The ships in this class are all named after states of the USA.

The nuclear submarine

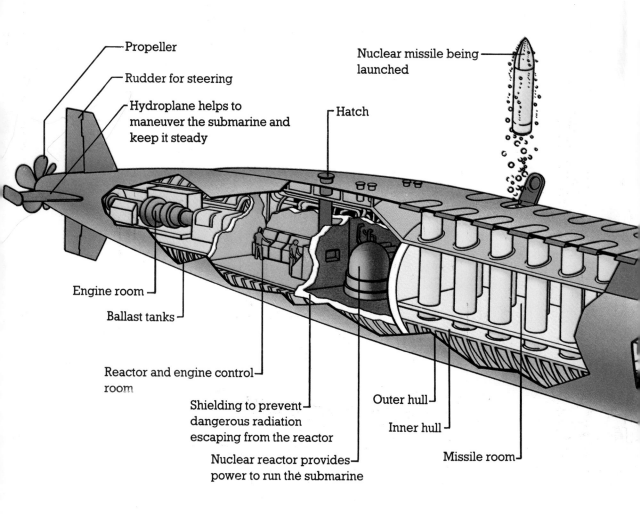

Propeller

Rudder for steering

Hydroplane helps to maneuver the submarine and keep it steady

Nuclear missile being launched

Hatch

Engine room

Ballast tanks

Reactor and engine control room

Shielding to prevent dangerous radiation escaping from the reactor

Nuclear reactor provides power to run the submarine

Outer hull

Inner hull

Missile room

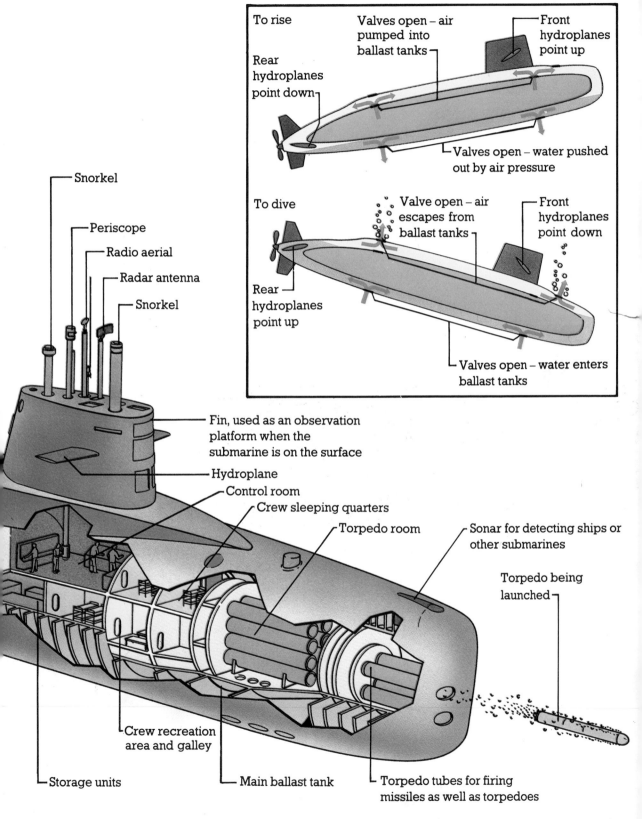

To rise

Valves open – air pumped into ballast tanks

Front hydroplanes point up

Rear hydroplanes point down

Valves open – water pushed out by air pressure

To dive

Valve open – air escapes from ballast tanks

Front hydroplanes point down

Rear hydroplanes point up

Valves open – water enters ballast tanks

Snorkel

Periscope

Radio aerial

Radar antenna

Snorkel

Fin, used as an observation platform when the submarine is on the surface

Hydroplane

Control room

Crew sleeping quarters

Torpedo room

Sonar for detecting ships or other submarines

Torpedo being launched

Crew recreation area and galley

Storage units

Main ballast tank

Torpedo tubes for firing missiles as well as torpedoes

Inside a submarine

The largest submarines have a crew of more than 150. On most submarines the crew on duty works in shifts or "watches" of four hours at a time. When this ends, the crew goes off duty.

The center of activity in a submarine is the control room. From here, the commander gives his orders, the submarine is steered and its weapons are fired.

▽ Inside the control room of a submarine. Red lighting is used at night to give the crew a sense of night and day. Otherwise, they would lose all sense of time and possibly become confused.

Instruments in the control room show the submarine's exact position at any time. Near the surface, the commander can use his periscope to search for surface vessels.

Switches in the control room are used to operate the engines and to show up any problems. The nuclear reactor is also monitored and all the missiles and weapons checked.

△ A submarine commander looks through his periscope in the control room. Modern periscopes have laser rangefinders and other advanced electronic aids.

△ The crewman in the center is one of the two "planesmen" who steers the submarine, using a control similar to a plane's joystick. On the left is a senior officer, in charge of operations.

◁ The nuclear reactor control room of *Le Redoutable*, a French ballistic missile submarine.

Nuclear submarines may be stationed in the ocean for weeks or months at a time. Sleeping quarters are made as comfortable as possible, but space is limited. Officers have cabins, while enlisted men share dormitories.

The crew is provided with good food and entertainment. Crew members can watch movies and play different kinds of games. On some submarines there are exercise machines.

△ The control panel for firing torpedoes on a hunter-killer submarine. The crewman on the left is at the manual controls of a torpedo tube and another tube can be seen below.

△ Preparing meals in a submarine's galley. Enough food must be stored to provide three meals a day for a crew of 120–150 for at least six weeks.

◁ Junior enlisted men eat lunch in a dining hall that is also used as a recreation space. The chief forms of entertainment are movies and videos.

Kinds of submarines

Nuclear-powered submarines can stay submerged under water for months at a time. They have equipment for making air and fresh water. They can move faster under water than on the surface.

Ballistic missile submarines are the largest of the underwater vessels. Some are $1\frac{1}{2}$ times the length of a football field. When submerged, some can travel at speeds of 30–40 knots (35–45 mph).

▽ USS *John C. Calhoun* is equipped to launch Poseidon ballistic missiles. Ballistic missile submarines spend very little time on the surface.

△ An artist's impression of the *Ohio* under water. Ballistic missile submarines spend nearly all of their tour of duty, about three months, submerged under water. The missiles have a range of 3,000 miles (5,000 km) or more.

◁ The missile tubes on the deck of a submarine, with hatches open.

Hunter-killer submarines are often attached to a fleet. They may serve as escorts, especially for aircraft carriers, to protect them from enemy submarine attacks.

Hunter-killers are also called fleet, or attack, submarines. They are armed with missiles and torpedoes for attacking enemy vessels. Some hunter-killers are also equipped for launching long-range, low-flying missiles.

▽ USS *Los Angeles* is a hunter-killer submarine. The *Los Angeles* came into service in 1976 and was the first in a class of more than thirty hunter-killers planned for the US Navy of the 1990s.

Diesel-electric submarines use their diesel engines to travel on the surface and to recharge their batteries. When submerged, they are powered by electricity from the batteries.

The chief task of diesel, or patrol, submarines is to attack enemy shipping. They are quiet and stealthy, but are not fast enough to operate with a fleet and must come to the surface for air.

◁ HMS *Superb*, a hunter-killer submarine of the British Royal Navy. The fin is used as an observation platform when the submarine is on the surface.

▽ A patrol submarine is smaller than a nuclear-powered vessel. Patrol submarines are useful in coastal waters because they are easier to maneuver in shallow water than the larger submarines.

◁ HMS *Walrus* is a patrol submarine of the British Royal Navy. It belongs to the Oberon class. Navies of countries as widespread as Australia, Canada and Brazil use these patrol submarines.

Oberon class submarines have a crew of about 70. They reach a top speed of about 16 knots under water and only 12 knots on the surface. By using a snorkel to take in fresh air when needed, they can remain under water for several weeks.

The weapons carried include 24 Tigerfish long-range anti-submarine torpedoes. The round structure at the front of the *Walrus* houses sonar equipment.

Submarine weapons

Submarines use many kinds of weapons, all of which are fired from under the water.

Torpedoes travel to their targets under water. Missiles are usually launched through torpedo tubes in containers which break open at the surface. The missiles are guided to their targets by radar. Ballistic missiles are ejected up through the surface of the water at great speed.

△ A submariner checks out a Harpoon anti-ship missile in a hunter-killer submarine. This type of missile is fired from a torpedo tube and it is guided low over the sea to its target.

▷ A Trident ballistic missile being test-fired. Tridents are launched under water, carry a nuclear warhead and have a very long range.

Anti-submarine weapons

Torpedoes and depth charges are the chief weapons used to destroy submarines. Torpedoes speed through the water and are guided to their target. Depth charges drop downward and are exploded at a pre-set depth.

These anti-submarine weapons may be launched from ships, planes, helicopters or other submarines.

Submarines are detected under water by means of sonar.

△ The Nimrod was specially built for anti-submarine warfare. It is packed with electronic equipment for detecting submarines. Its chief method is to drop sonar buoys on to the surface of the water and then pick up signals from them.

▷ The helicopter is searching for submarines by dipping sonar. The sonar device is dangled in the water and sends signals back to the helicopter.

Submersibles

Most submersibles are small craft, either unmanned or with a crew of two to four. The unmanned, or robot, craft are controlled from "mother" ships or oil rigs.

Submersibles are used in the offshore oil-drilling industry, in salvage work and for scientific research. Other uses include checking pipelines and cables.

▽ A manned submersible is launched from its special support vessel. A crew of three or four can operate in comfort inside it. The submersible is used for surveying the sea bed before pipelines are laid.

△ Inside a
submersible, a
crewman is surrounded
by dials and controls.
Through the window, a
diver can be seen
working on the sea
bed.

▷ A submersible on
the surface of the
water ready to make a
dive.

The story of submarines

The first submarines

Boats intended to operate under the water were first designed some 400 years ago. The first workable craft was a rowing boat covered with waterproof hide. Its inventor, a Dutchman called Cornelius von Drebel, demonstrated it in England in about 1620.

But it was not until 1776, during the Revolutionary War, that a submarine was first used in warfare. This was a one-man craft called the *Turtle*, powered by a propeller cranked by hand. It was designed by David Bushnell, a student at Yale University. The *Turtle* failed in an attempt to sink a British warship in New York harbor.

△ An A-class submarine, A2, of the early 1900s.

The first victims

In 1864, during the American Civil War, a submersible craft called the *Hunley* was used by Confederates to attack the Union ironclad steamship *Housatonic* off Charleston, South Carolina. The *Hunley* rammed the *Housatonic* with a torpedo attached to a long pole, but the explosion sent both vessels to the bottom of the harbor.

Submarines in the Navy

In the 1890s, an American inventor, John P. Holland, designed a submarine that ran on a petrol engine on the surface and electric batteries under water. The US Navy bought it in 1900 and called it the USS *Holland*. It was 53 ft (16 m) long and had a speed of 5 knots under water.

More Holland class submarines were commissioned by the US Navy and also by Britain's Royal Navy. The British began to develop the submarine. From the A class, first launched in 1902, to the D class (1911), nearly 70 submarines were built.

The deadly U-boats

Until World War I (1914–18), submarines were still regarded as unreliable "toys," but the deadly U-boats of the German

△ A mine-laying U-boat captured by the British in World War I.

Navy changed all this.

The "U" stands for Untersee, or "under-sea". The U1 was launched in 1905.

The Germans built more powerful U-boats, many of them designed for laying mines. During the war they launched more than 350 U-boats, and their submarine fleet became the terror of the seas. In 1915, a U-boat torpedoed and sank the *Lusitania*, a British liner with many Americans aboard. The United States entered the war in 1917, after a series of U-boat attacks on her merchant ships.

War under the seas

In World War II (1939–45), most of the major navies used submarines. German U-boats operated in the Atlantic Ocean, stopping vital supplies reaching Britain from the USA. British submarines in the Mediterranean Sea prevented German and Italian shipping taking supplies to their troops in North Africa. And US submarines destroyed the Japanese merchant fleet in the Pacific Ocean.

△ HMS *Pandora*, built in 1930.

The nuclear threat

The first nuclear-powered submarine was the *Nautilus*, launched by the US Navy in 1954. The first ballistic missile submarines came into service with the US Navy in the early 1960s. They carried Polaris missiles, capable of hitting a target 1,250 miles (2,000 km) away. Britain, France and the Soviet Union now have ballistic missile submarines. They stay under the seas and are a deadly threat to any opposing power, making war too dangerous to start. This is called deterrence.

Facts and records

Under the North Pole

In 1958 the US nuclear-powered submarine *Nautilus* became the first to sail under the ice at the North Pole.

Around the world

In 1960, the USS *Triton* became the first submarine to sail completely around the world under water. It took 84 days to make the journey of 41,500 miles (66,790 km).

Deadly weapons

The destructive power of the nuclear warheads carried in a single ballistic missile submarine is more than all the bombs and shells used by all sides in World War II.

△ Lafayette-class submarines, although much smaller than those in the Ohio class, have a larger crew of 168 compared with 133.

Biggest

The world's biggest submarines belong to the Soviet Typhoon class. The Soviet government does not release details of its latest military craft, but it is known that the first of this class of ballistic missile submarine was launched in 1980. It is believed to measure nearly 590 ft (180 m) in length.

△ A midget submarine built in the mid-1950s, the X51. In World War II, the British developed X-craft to plant explosive charges under ships at anchor. They destroyed the German battleship *Tirpitz* in this way.

△ The biggest submarines are the ballistic missile craft. The USS *Ohio* is 560 ft (170.7 m) long.

Glossary

Ballistic missile submarine
A nuclear submarine armed with long-range nuclear missiles.

Fin
The structure that houses the periscopes and aerials.

Hull
The body or frame of a vessel. Submarines have an inner and an outer hull.

Hunter-killer
A nuclear submarine used to attack the enemy and to protect its own fleet.

Hydroplanes
Control surfaces used for maneuvering the submarine.

Knot
A nautical mile per hour. One nautical mile equals 6076.1 feet (1.852 km).

Nuclear reactor
A generator that produces power by means of atomic reactions.

Nuclear submarine
Any submarine that runs on nuclear power.

Patrol submarine
A small submarine that runs on diesel fuel.

Periscope
A device used to see above the surface of the water while the submarine is submerged.

Snorkel
A tube used to draw in fresh air while the submarine is under water. In diesel submarines, the snorkel also gets rid of engine fumes.

Sonar (Sound Navigation and Ranging)
A method used for detecting submarines under water by means of sound echoes.

Submariner
A submarine sailor.

Submersible
A kind of mini-sub, unmanned or with a small crew.

Warhead
The explosive charge carried by a torpedo or missile.

Watch
A set period of duty, usually of four hours.

Index